7 days in Sept. / Oct

SUKKOT
A TIME TO REJOICE

"The Sukkah" by Moritz Oppenheim, Germany, 1865
ISRAEL MUSEUM, JERUSALEM

a JEWISH HOLIDAYS book

SUKKOT
A TIME TO REJOICE

by Malka Drucker
drawings by Brom Hoban

HOLIDAY HOUSE · NEW YORK

OTHER JEWISH HOLIDAYS BOOKS

Hanukkah: Eight Nights, Eight Lights
Passover: A Season of Freedom
Rosh Hashanah and Yom Kippur: Sweet Beginnings

For Bonnie Jo

Copyright © 1982 by Malka Drucker
All rights reserved
Printed in the United States of America
First Edition

Library of Congress Cataloging in Publication Data

Drucker, Malka.
    Sukkot, a time to rejoice.

    (A Jewish holidays book)
    Bibliography: p.
    Includes index.
    Summary: Discusses the longest and happiest holiday
season in the Jewish year, and explains the customs, history, and meaning connected with it. Includes games, reci-
pes, puzzles, crafts, and a glossary of terms.
    1. Sukkoth—Juvenile literature. [1. Suk-
koth] I. Hoban, Brom, ill. II. Title. III. Series.
BM695.S8D78   296.4′33   82-80814
ISBN 0-8234-0466-8   AACR2

ACKNOWLEÐGMENTS

The author would like to thank the following people for helping with the manuscript: Vicky Kelman, Rabbi Harold M. Schulweis, Dr. Yona Sabar, and Ivan Matthew Drucker. Special thanks to the Sinai Temple Library and its patient, supportive staff.

She would also like to thank:

Farrar, Straus & Giroux, Inc., for granting permission to reprint an excerpt from *Reaches of Heaven* by Isaac Bashevis Singer, illustrated by Ira Moskowitz. Text copyright © 1980 by Isaac Bashevis Singer.

The Jewish Publication Society of America for permission to reprint Torah portions from the JPS Torah.

Michael Strassfeld for permission to reprint the prayer welcoming the Ushpizin.

ABOUT THE PHOTO CREDITS

Skirball Museum is short for Hebrew Union College Skirball Museum, Los Angeles.

Yivo is short for "from the archives of the Yivo Institute for Jewish Research."

JTS is short for the Jewish Theological Seminary of America.

CONTENTS

TO THE READER

Sukkot is a fall harvest festival celebrated by Jews all over the world. Unlike other Jewish festivals, it requires that a special place be built for its celebration. While other holidays simply need a day or two set aside and people to observe them, Sukkot must be observed in a handmade shack or hut called a *sukkah.*

When you step into the sukkah, it is like stepping out of the twentieth century and going back to a time when people lived close to nature and respected and appreciated the delicate balance of the seasons. For people today, Sukkot offers a yearly opportunity to camp out in a sukkah and to remember that they are part of the natural world.

Some holidays, such as the *High Holy Days,* have meanings that are mysterious and deep. Others, like *Passover,* need much historical explanation to be understood. Sukkot, however, is wonderfully simple. Its chief mood is one of happiness and the sharing of this happiness with friends and family. In fact, Sukkot has another name, *Zeman Simhatenu,* which means "Season of Our Joy."

Even simple Jewish holidays have many meanings. I hope that this book will help to explain the holiday's connections to the past, its meaning for the present, and its wish for the time when all people will sit together in the *Sukkat Shalom,* the great Shelter of Peace.

18th-century English engraving of "The Feasts
and Rejoicings of the Jews during the Feast
of Tabernacles" (in ancient times)   JTS

I

CLOUDS OF GLORY

*You shall rejoice in your festival [Sukkot],
with your son and daughter, your male
and female slave, the* Levite, *the stranger
and fatherless, and the widow in your
communities. You shall hold the festival
for God seven days in the place that the
Lord will choose. For the Lord your God
will bless all your crops and all your un-
dertakings, and you shall have nothing but
joy.*

DEUTERONOMY 16:14–15

Sukkot, which begins on the eve of the fifteenth of *Tishri*
(in September or early October) and ends nine days later
with *Simhat Torah,* is the longest and happiest holiday
season of the Jewish year. This autumn festival is celebrated in a fragile but richly decorated little house
called a sukkah. The first two days are full holidays. No
one goes to school or work, there are special synagogue

11

services, and friends and families share delicious meals in the sukkah. The next five days, which are called *Hol ha-Moed,* are also celebrated in the synagogue and sukkah, but people go to work and school as usual. The last two days, *Shemini Atzeret* and Simhat Torah, are full holidays that end the fall holiday season with a climax of festivities.

The reason the first two days of Sukkot are full holidays is that the Jewish calendar is based partly on the phases of the moon. Twenty-two hundred years ago, the new month began when the new moon appeared. The rabbis sent runners throughout Israel to announce the new month. When the new moon of Tishri appeared, every Jew living near Jerusalem knew that Sukkot would begin fifteen days later. But after the Temple, the holy place where all Jews prayed, was destroyed in the year 70 C.E., the Jewish people were scattered throughout the world, and the runners could no longer reach everyone. Since the new moon can occur on the twenty-ninth or thirtieth day of the month, the rabbis made most festivals outside Israel last for two days instead of one. That way, everyone would be sure to cele-

"Blessing of the Moon," handwritten on parchment
ISRAEL MUSEUM, JERUSALEM

brate the holiday on the right day. In Israel, only the first and eighth days of Sukkot are full holidays, and Shemini Atzeret and Simhat Torah are celebrated on the same day.

The *Hasidim,* the mystical Eastern European Jews of the eighteenth century, found another reason for a two-day observance of Sukkot. Since generosity is one of the most important parts of this holiday, the Hasidim explained, "On the first day of each festival, God extends us an invitation to observe a day of rejoicing with Him; on the second day, we invite Him to rejoice with us! God commanded us to observe the first day of the festival; the second day, we [the Jewish people] instituted ourselves."

Sukkot celebrates both history and nature. When the Jewish people were freed from slavery in Egypt three thousand years ago, they didn't live a life of comfort and ease right away. After leaving behind the cruel and bitter days of Egypt, the Israelites wandered in the wilderness. There were no trees to protect them from the fierce desert sun, and many wondered if they would survive. With only a vague idea of where they would find the land that God had promised them, some doubted that they were truly better off by being free. Only the children, who were born in the desert and had never been slaves, were hopeful.

The *Torah,* the first five books of the Bible, explains that the Israelites lived in booths, under God's protection, for forty years in the desert. Since this happened thousands of years ago, no one knows exactly what these booths looked like. Rabbi Eliezer, a great teacher in the first century C.E., believed that the *sukkot*—which is the plural of sukkah in Hebrew and means booths or *taber-nacles*—were not real buildings, but seven clouds created by God to protect the people from the searing heat of the desert. One cloud was under their feet as a carpet, one was over their heads as a shadow, four surrounded them as four walls, and the last cloud led the way. Rabbi Eliezer thought that these were the "clouds of glory" described in Isaiah 4:5–6.

When the Jewish people finally saw the land that God had promised them, they were overjoyed. It was lush with fruits and vegetables, had rich soil, and flowed with rivers and streams. The Jews became farmers and grew olives, wheat, and grapes for wine. When it was time for the harvest in the early fall, they built little wooden huts near their crops and lived in them until they had finished the harvesting of the field. They needed to be near the crops to pick them quickly and to protect them from a sudden storm. From the first light of day to the first star of evening, they gathered their crops. For this reason, Sukkot is also call *Hag ha-Asif*, the Festival of the

A sukkah from the *Book of Customs*, Amsterdam, 1723
ISRAEL MUSEUM, JERUSALEM

Ingathering. It was the final gathering-in of fruits, vegetables, and grains. In time, Sukkot became a celebration of both the harvest and the forty-year wandering. The sukkah became a symbol of protection and peace, and the holiday became a time of feasting and of thanking God for the harvest.

If this holiday sounds like Thanksgiving, it may be no coincidence. After the Pilgrims survived their first year in America, they wanted to celebrate and thank God for the food they grew in the strange new country. Some historians think that because the Pilgrims knew about Sukkot from the Bible, they modeled the first Thanksgiving feast after it. Like the Jews, the Pilgrims were not only grateful for the food that they had, but were also thankful for God's protection in the new land. The first Thanksgiving celebration fell in October and lasted for three days.

Even though today most Jews are not farmers, they still celebrate Sukkot. It has become more than just a harvest festival, for the mood of the holiday has meaning for everyone: the joy in well-being and in completion, and the relief that comes with finishing a hard task. *Rosh Hashanah* and *Yom Kippur,* the High Holy Days that fall two weeks before Sukkot and mark the beginning of the Jewish year, require the difficult work of self-examination and repentance. Sukkot is like the "harvest" of these deeply serious holidays: a new self starting fresh. It's a time to give thanks, feel satisfied, and have well-earned fun.

The season of the High Holy Days begins with introspection and solemnity and ends with the joy of Sukkot. Sadness is forbidden on Sukkot. The *Ba'al Shem Tov,* the greatest Hasidic master, said, "He who is full of joy is full of love for human beings and all fellow creatures." In other words, you can only help someone else to feel happy if you yourself know what happiness feels like. Of course, the feeling of being happy is not reserved only for Sukkot, but Sukkot is a special time set aside for remembering that joy is holy.

On a day during Sukkot, usually on *Shabbat,* the book of *Ecclesiastes* is read in the synagogues. This book, which is part of the Bible, teaches that there is a time for everything: "To every thing there is a season, and a time to every purpose under heaven: a time to be born, and a time to heal; a time to break down, and a time to build up; a time to weep, and a time to laugh; a time to mourn, and a time to dance; a time to cast away stones, and a time to gather stones; a time to seek, and a time to lose; a time to keep, and a time to cast away; a time to rend, and a time to sew; a time to keep silence, and a time to speak; a time to love, and a time to hate; a time for war, and a time for peace."

There are four plants that are essential to Sukkot. They are described in the Torah (Leviticus 23:40): "On the first day you shall take the fruit of goodly trees, branches of palm trees, boughs of leafy trees, and willows of the brook, and you shall rejoice before the Lord your God seven days." In Hebrew these plants are called *arba'ah minim,* the "four species." Each is different from the other, and each has its own meaning.

The *lulav* is a tall green palm branch. It was a national emblem of ancient Israel. Its tall and straight leaf represents righteousness.

Three sprigs of *hadasim,* shiny myrtle leaves, are tied

The roof of a sukkah (sekhakh) made from palm fronds   BILL ARON

Buying aravot on
the lower East Side
of New York
IRVING I. HERZBERG

Choosing an etrog before Sukkot   BILL ARON

to the right side of the lulav, and two sprigs of *aravot,* delicate willow, are tied to the left. The willow, which grows by streams, is a reminder of life-giving water. Some people believe the myrtle is the plant Adam and Eve took from the Garden of Eden. It grew and flowered on earth and is a reminder of the world to come.

Strands of the lulav are used to bind these three plants together. Sometimes all three are called "lulav," because it is the most prominent.

The fourth plant, the *etrog,* or citron, looks like a large, lumpy lemon. This ancient fruit may have been the fruit of knowledge in the Garden of Eden.

Maimonides, a great medieval philosopher, said that the four species express the joy of the Jews' having journeyed from the barren desert to the land of rivers and trees. The rabbis compared the fragrances and tastes of the plants and said that the arba'ah minim also stand for types of human behavior. "Taste" and "common sense" are the same word in Hebrew: *ta'am*. The rabbis often spoke of the "fragrance of good deeds." This fragrance spreads and remains undiminished, no matter how many it touches. Just as two hundred people can smell one bag of fresh popcorn, two hundred people can benefit from one person's kindness.

The lulav has no fragrance, but because it is the leaf of the palm tree that bears dates, it does have taste. The myrtle branches have no taste but have a wonderful fragrance. The willow has neither taste nor fragrance. Finally, the etrog possesses both fragrance and taste. In this way, the lulav is like the person who is learned but doesn't do good deeds; the myrtle is like the person who is ignorant but kind to others; the willow is like the person who is neither learned nor does good deeds; and the etrog is like the person who is both learned and kind. These four belong together because the world needs everyone.

The arba'ah minim also symbolize a human body. The lulav stands for the backbone, or strength; the myrtle for the eyes, or enlightenment; the willow for the lips, or prayer; and the etrog for the heart, or understanding. The rabbis said the heart was the most difficult but most important part to bring to a holiday. It is the heart that completes the prayer. When you hold the four plants together, they represent your entire self serving God. Psalm 35 says, "All my limbs shall say, O Lord, who is like unto thee?"

The following story, which plays with the double meaning of the etrog as a fruit and a heart, illustrates the

These people are getting ready to bless
the arba'ah minim.   BILL ARON

importance of wholeness on Sukkot. Two men of Helm, a town known for its outrageously stupid people, could not afford separately to buy a lulav and etrog for Sukkot, so they went into partnership and bought them together. But this soon proved to be an unsatisfactory solution, for they immediately began to argue about who would have the honor of making the first blessing. The rabbi, the only wise person in Helm, overheard them. "Stop fighting," he said. "I'll settle this." Quickly taking a knife in his hand, he cut the etrog right down the middle and handed each man a half. Both men were horrified. The etrog was worthless now, because it must be whole to fulfill the *mitzvah,* or commandment, of Sukkot. The story also shows that the heart, too, must be whole to perform a mitzvah; it cannot be done half-heartedly.

Since the Torah says that it is a mitzvah to celebrate Sukkot with beauty, the choosing of the arba'ah minim, which usually come from Israel, is a careful business. You can buy a lulav and an etrog at a Jewish bookstore or a synagogue. Many people go into partnership with the synagogue, because most synagogues buy sets to be shared by the people who come to the Sukkot service. When choosing the arba'ah minim, everyone gives special attention to the etrog. It must be whole, with the blossom end, or *pittum,* attached and it should be fresh, fat, and shiny. The rabbis knew, however, that the richest people can always buy the best, and there is a temptation for people to feel that the more beautiful the etrog, the greater their mitzvah.

To discourage that kind of thinking, the rabbis sometimes told a story about a very poor Jewish community in Eastern Europe. The village was so poor that it could afford only one lulav and one etrog for everyone. The rabbi collected all the money and set out for the nearest city to buy the arba'ah minim. Along the way, he heard deep sobs coming from the woods. He followed the sound until he came upon a man crying beside a dead horse. The rabbi asked him what was wrong. "This horse was my life," the man said. "I'm a delivery man, and this horse and I have traveled many miles together. He just dropped dead and now I am finished. How will I feed my family?" he moaned.

The rabbi thought a moment and asked, "How much does a new horse cost?"

"Fifty *shekels,*" the man replied. This was exactly the amount the rabbi was carrying to buy the lulav and etrog. Without a moment's hesitation, he reached into his pocket and handed the man the money.

The rabbi returned to his village, where the people crowded around him expectantly. "Where are the lulav and etrog?" they asked. When he told them the story of the man and his horse, they were shocked. "How could you do this? What will we make the blessing with? This is terrible!" they all shouted at him.

"Listen," said the rabbi, raising his hands to quiet them. "The whole world is going to make a blessing over a lulav and an etrog; but *we* are going to make a blessing over a dead horse!"

If the mitzvah of Sukkot is joy, the most joyful way to obey God's laws is *tzedakah,* helping those in need.

There is a special morning service in the synagogue for every day of Sukkot. People bring their arba'ah minim to use during the service. First they make this blessing over the four plants: "Blessed are You, Lord our God, Ruler of the Universe, who sanctified us with His commandments and has commanded us concerning the waving of the lulav." During the prayer, they hold the lulav in the right hand, with its spine facing the body, and the etrog in the left hand, with the pittum pointing down. On the first day they add a prayer of thanksgiving: "Blessed are You, Lord our God, King of the Universe, who has granted us life and sustenance and permitted us to reach this season."

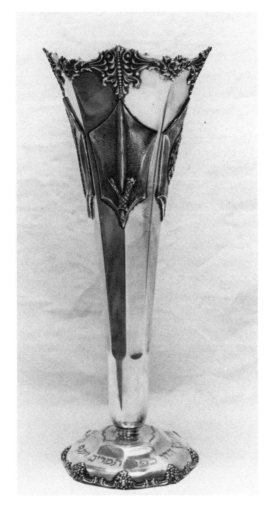

Silver lulav holder
MORIAH, ANTIQUES-JUDAICA

The arba'ah minim are now ready for the *Hallel,* the reciting of Psalms 113–118. The etrog is turned so that the pittum is on top, and moved to touch the lulav. The lulav is shaken while the following words are recited: "Praise the Lord, for He is good, for His steadfast love is forever" (Psalm 118:1). The lulav and etrog are made to touch each other to express the unity of the Jewish people and the wholeness of the self. The lulav is shaken and pointed in six directions to show that God is everywhere. But when the name of God is said in the prayer, the lulav is not moved, because God is the unshakable center of the universe. Also, six directions plus one person equal seven, which is the number of completion in the Jewish tradition.

The Torah reading, which tells of the laws of Sukkot, follows the Hallel. Part of it reads:

Mark, on the fifteenth day of the seventh month, when you have gathered in the yield of your land, you shall observe the festival of the Lord to last seven days: a complete rest on the first day and complete rest on the eighth day. On the first day you shall take the products of goodly trees, branches of palm trees, boughs of leafy trees, and willows of the brook, and you shall rejoice before the Lord your God seven days. You shall observe it as a festival of the Lord for seven days in the year; you shall observe it in the seventh month as a law for all time, throughout the ages. You shall live in booths, in order that future generations may know that I made the Israelite people live in booths when I brought them out of the land of Egypt, I the Lord your God. (Leviticus 23:39–43)

After the Torah reading, the Torah is not returned to the holy ark right away. Instead, someone carries the Torah around the congregation, followed by the rabbi and the cantor. Everyone with a lulav and an etrog joins in the parade. This circling is accompanied by exclamations of *Hoshanah!* ("O Save Us!"), which is a plea for life-giving water in the coming months. Many people put the *tallit*, or prayer shawl, over their heads during the procession, a custom that dates back to the days of the ancient Temple.

Being in a synagogue filled with people holding the arba'ah minim is an amazing experience. You feel as if you've wandered into a field of moving corn. When the lulav is shaken, its sound is like the sighing of wind through the trees. For a moment, the sound seems to carry you back to a time when the Jewish people, in a simple yet profound way, thanked God for the harvest of their fields.

Procession in synagogue with etrog and lulav; engraved by J. Herz
JTS

2

INVISIBLE GUESTS

It is necessary for you to rejoice within the sukkah and to show a cheerful countenance to guests. It is forbidden to harbor thoughts of gloom, and how much more so feelings of anger within the sukkah, the symbol of joy.

Zohar

Jewish people today build sukkot to remember both their ancestors' huts in the desert and the farmers' harvest shacks in ancient Israel; but there is another, more immediate meaning of the sukkah. Even though the sukkah may be beautiful and fun to live in, it is only a temporary place, like a sand castle. The wind blows through the sukkah and it provides no protection from the rain. Some people mistake their power and think that they can control everything in their lives. They may build a strong house to protect themselves from life's dangers. A

26

mudslide or a fire is a terrible reminder that this isn't possible for anyone. Maimonides believed that the sukkah was a lesson in human frailty. No matter how self-reliant we may be, we are still vulnerable to the forces of nature.

The joy of the sukkah is mixed with the memory of the barren, burning desert. Sukkot is celebrated at the end of the harvest, when the weather is already turning cold. June would be a much more pleasant month in which to celebrate Sukkot, but it would not have the autumn air's sharpness to remind you that winter is coming. Winter, like the desert, is often barren.

Just as the *matzah* eaten on Passover is humble and plain, the sukkah is a reminder that a simple life is best. Thousands of years after the wilderness experience, the rabbis reflected that the years of wandering had much good in them. Despite the harshness, it was a pure time when everyone lived in the same way with enough, but not more than enough. Wild plants and animals are

Modern sukkah in upstate New York   BILL ARON

stronger than cultivated species because they survive with little help from the environment. People grow strong in a harsh place, too. Spending a week in a sukkah is not a pioneering experience, but the contrast between the simple sukkah and a comfortable house may make you wonder if you really need all the appliances and gadgets in your house. Maybe you'd feel stronger with fewer of them.

Being in a sukkah makes you think about other things, too. The sukkah may be fun to camp out in for a week, but would you want to stay in one for a year? Poverty forces some people to live in shacks all the time. Unless you have experienced this for yourself, you cannot know how uncomfortable and difficult it can be. Just as the sukkah is not a closed building, so people must not close themselves off from the suffering of other people. The sukkah surrounds and envelops you on all sides, but its roof allows you to keep in touch with the outside. Its openness permits you to look at the full moon and stars—at the world outside yourself—and is a reminder of human vulnerability.

The days between Yom Kippur and Sukkot are exciting. No one wastes time getting started on making the sukkot. In fact, the rabbis said to begin driving in the first post moments after Yom Kippur ends. The idea is to go "from strength to strength."

You can build the walls of the sukkah out of any material, or you can use an already existing structure for your sukkah. The important thing is that the sukkah must have a *sekhakh*, a temporary roof of leafy branches. In the eighteenth century, some wealthy European Jews found an easy solution for creating a sukkah. They had a

"Sukkot on Rooftops"; engraved by unknown 18th-century German artist ISRAEL MUSEUM, JERUSALEM

little room in the house that served as an ordinary room throughout the year. But when Sukkot came, the roof, which was on hinges, could be lifted up and disappeared as if by magic, creating an instant sukkah! This arrangement may have met the requirements of the law, but perhaps it did not fulfill the spirit of Sukkot. The rabbis said that every year, when you take down the sukkah and put the parts away, you hope that you won't have to build the sukkah next year. This is not because of laziness, but because you wish that the next year will be the time when all the world will sit together in peace.

In addition to performing the mitzvah of building the sukkah, you must eat at least two meals in it. The first meal takes place on 15 Tishri, the first night of Sukkot. (All Jewish holidays begin at sundown, because, just as wandering comes before finding and planting comes before sowing, so darkness comes before light.) The dinner table inside the sukkah is often splendid. It may be set for many more people than the family. There is often a beautiful centerpiece, such as a bowl of grapes, apples, and pomegranates. Brass candlesticks, silver wine cups for everyone, and the sweet-smelling holiday bread called *hallah* draws everyone into the sukkah.

It's customary to invite many guests to help fulfill the mitzvah of dwelling in the sukkah. The building is a symbol of joy not only for yourself or for the Jewish people, but for everyone. So it's a fine time to invite lots of people, regardless of whether or not they themselves celebrate Sukkot.

Hospitality is always a mitzvah, but it is an essential part of Sukkot. For one thing, it is the first opportunity of the new year to be caring and kind. It is a special mitzvah to invite the poor, because the rabbis said the poor reflect the image of God. The people you invite will eat the food prepared for the *Ushpizin*—invisible guests "who see but who are not seen." The Ushpizin are the seven patriarchs and seven matriarchs, who are invited into the sukkah. Each night one patriarch and one matriarch are specifically welcomed, but extra food is not set out unless real people are invited. The sukkah is decorated with colorful posters picturing the Ushpizin, along with these special prayers for Sukkot:

> May it be Your will, Lord my God, and God of my ancestors, to cause the *Shekhinah* [Divine Presence] to dwell in our midst. Spread over us Your shelter of peace by virtue of our fulfillment of the mitzvah of Sukkah. Surround us with the light of Your Holy Glory. May it spread over our heads as an eagle that stirs in its nest.

> To remember the path of wandering, I have left the comfort of my home, to eat in this sukkah. So, too, do I

Festival table inside sukkah   STEPHANIE SABAR

remember the commandment of hospitality for the poor, the hungry, and the stranger. May we soon see the fulfillment of the words of the prophet Amos: "Behold, there will come a time when God will send a famine into the land; not a hunger for food or a thirst for water, but rather a hunger to hear the words of the Lord."

I invite the illustrious guests to my table: Abraham, Isaac, Jacob, Joseph, Moses, Aaron, and David. Sarah, Rebecca, Rachel, Leah, Miriam, Hannah, and Deborah.

On the first night say: Abraham, you are welcome to join us; welcome, too, are all the illustrious guests: Isaac, Jacob, Joseph, Moses, Aaron, and David. Sarah, you are welcome to join us; welcome, too, are all the illustrious guests: Rebecca, Rachel, Leah, Miriam, Hannah, and Deborah.

The invisible guests are invited into the sukkah because they were wanderers and because of their importance in Jewish history. David, the last patriarch to be invited, has special significance on Sukkot. He was a king of Israel, and the Jewish people believe that the Messiah will be his descendant. Because David was a graceful musician and poet, some people put a musical instrument in their sukkah. David's link to the Messiah connects him to the time when all nations of the world will sit in peace under the Sukkat Shalom, which will be made of the skin of a *leviathan*, a supernatural sea creature. As they feast together eating the meat of the leviathan, they will rejoice in the Messiah's arrival. How will they know the Messiah is here? By seeing that everyone has enough to eat and that all nations are one. "On that day the Lord shall be One and His name will be One."

The following Hasidic tale illustrates the importance

of hospitality. Zuzya was a learned man who was often asked for advice on matters ranging from *kosher* foods to the settling of arguments. He might have been pleased that he was so much respected, but instead he resented the many interruptions by people wanting to question him. It kept him from his studies, which he believed were far more important than people's questions.

One day, when Zuzya was deeply immersed in his books, a woman came into his study holding a chicken. She wanted to know if it had been slaughtered correctly, according to Jewish law. "That does it!" he thought angrily. Shooing the woman away, he immediately prayed to God to be left alone to pursue his work. No one came to see him, and he was content.

When the High Holy Days came, Zuzya fasted and prayed harder than anyone. Right after Yom Kippur, he asked some of his neighbors to help him build a sukkah. In the *shtetl* where he lived, the custom was for people to build sukkot together. But since God had granted Zuzya's prayer to be left alone, no one would help him.

"Very well," he said, "I'll build it myself." So he got out some wood and nails and built his sukkah. The first night he entered his sukkah alone, because he had not invited any guests. He said his prayers and then invited Abraham into the sukkah. But Abraham would not enter: "I cannot come into a sukkah where no one else is welcome," the patriarch said.

Zuzya now realized that doing the rituals and saying the prayers are meaningless unless you understand what they teach. Zuzya had missed the whole point of Sukkot. Zuzya then asked God to revoke his prayer, and once again he welcomed his neighbors to his house.

On the first night of Sukkot everyone enters the sukkah expectantly. Even if you've been working on building and decorating it all week, it still is surprisingly
lovely on that first night. You light the candles with the
following blessing: "Blessed are You, Lord Our God,
who has commanded us to light the holiday candles."
Then you welcome the Ushpizin with the special prayer,
and you also welcome your visible guests to a festive
meal. Everyone says the *kiddush* and *ha-motzi*, the
blessings over the meal. (See Appendix.) Fruits and vegetables, bits of sky peeking between leaves of the sekhakh, a mysterious sense of the Ushpizin's presence, and
the shared pleasure of celebrating with friends and family all add up to make Sukkot the happiest of holidays.

Ushpizin poster   JTS

3

APPLES, FLAGS, AND RAIN

And there was very great gladness.

At the beginning of September, Jews look forward to the excitement of the holiday season, and by the end of the month, they are not disappointed. Out of the twenty-four-day period between Rosh Hashanah and Simhat Torah, twelve days are set aside as holidays, and joy is the predominant mood.

One of those days is *Hoshanah Rabbah,* which falls on the seventh day of Sukkot. Although the holiday is a happy one, it suggests the beginning of the season's end. It's been such a good holiday that no one wants to put away the sweet-smelling etrog and dismantle the sukkah.

The evening of Hoshanah Rabbah is filled with mystery. Everyone who can stays up all night studying and praying together. This is called a *tikkun.* Some people believe that the heavens open that night, and that if you make a wish then, it will come true. Some people also believe that if you see your shadow on Hoshanah Rabbah and it is missing the head, you will die within the year.

The following morning, everyone brings the lulav and etrog to the synagogue. Instead of circling the room only once with the arba'ah minim, they circle it seven times, each time saying "Hoshanah!" To understand what the ceremony means, it's helpful to remember that this ancient ritual goes back to a time when the Jews were an agricultural people. The bounty of the year depends upon rain, and Israel is a dry land. Therefore, the *Hoshanot* are like rain dances. The ceremony is also a last-minute plea for God's forgiveness, because Hoshanah Rabbah was the very last chance to do *teshuvah,* if you hadn't done it on Yom Kippur. Teshuvah means facing up to your wrongdoings, asking forgiveness, and starting fresh. After the seven Hoshanot, everyone beats the willow attached to the lulav until all its leaves fall. This is to encourage rain, since willows grow by the fertile banks of streams, and the fallen leaves are like raindrops. The end of Hoshanah Rabbah is the last time the lulav and etrog are used for the holiday. Some people save the etrog for its fragrance and the lulav for sweeping up bread crumbs on Passover.

The eighth day of Sukkot is Shemini Atzeret, a full holiday. Shemini Atzeret is really the mystery holiday of the Jewish year. No one can say precisely what it means, and even those who know find it hard to explain its importance. Perhaps this is because the meaning is so simple that it escapes someone who is looking for the rich

PROCESSION des PALMES chez les JUIFS PORTUGAIS.

REPAS des JUIFS pendant la FÊTE des TENTES.

Hashanot and a Sukkot feast by Bernard Picart,
1724, Amsterdam   ISRAEL MUSEUM, JERUSALEM

and complicated meanings that most Jewish holidays have. The clue to Shemini Atzeret is the word "atzeret," which means "tarry" in Hebrew. The holiday is an extra day added to Sukkot for no other reason than to lengthen the joy of it. Everyone wants the joy of the season to tarry, or stay, so Shemini Atzeret is a way of saying, "Stay a day longer."

In Israel, people leave the sukkah the day before, on Hoshanah Rabbah. Then they enjoy Shemini Atzeret in the comfort of their homes instead of in a flimsy sukkah. In other parts of the world, however, people eat dinner and lunch in the sukkah on Shemini Atzeret, but they don't say the usual blessing for being there. After lunch, they leave the sukkah for the last time and say good-bye to it with the following prayer: "May it be Your will, Lord our God and God of our fathers and mothers, that as I have been privileged to fulfill Thy commandment and have dwelt in this sukkah, so in the future may I be privileged to dwell in the sukkah made of the leviathan."

The morning synagogue service includes two special prayers after the Torah reading. The first, *Yizkor,* is in memory of relatives and friends who have died. This is another reminder of human frailty. During periods of great joy, the rabbis wanted people to remember that all times are temporary, including good ones. The second prayer is the prayer for *geshem,* which means "rain" in Hebrew. (You don't say this prayer during Sukkot, because rain in the sukkah is no fun!) Even if it is pouring rain while you recite the geshem prayer, you still say it as a reminder of Israel and its needs.

The last day of the holiday cycle, Simhat Torah, is the

most exuberant celebration of the year. The Hasidim said that during the High Holy Day season, you serve God with your whole being. On Rosh Hashanah you serve with your brain, because memory is so important, and on Yom Kippur you serve Him with your heart. On Sukkot you serve with your hands by building the sukkah, and on the last, or ninth, day of Sukkot, you serve with your feet when you march with the Torah.

Simhat Torah, which means "Rejoicing in the Torah," began a thousand years ago, but the ceremony as it is performed today began during the Middle Ages.

Dancing in the street during Simhat Torah   IRVING I. HERZBERG

Anyone who thinks that devotion to the Torah is always solemn and serious would be astounded at Simhat Torah. It is a joyful and sometimes boisterous celebration in honor of a book that has been read and reread for three thousand years and still speaks to every generation and every person. On Shabbat the Jewish people sing of the Torah: "It is a Tree of Life to those that hold fast to it." Even the letters in the Torah are holy. Each letter represents a soul on earth. The *mystics* said that each letter also has a deep, symbolic meaning.

On Simhat Torah, the reading of the Torah, which has been continued each week, is completed. The joy comes not only from finishing the book but also from the pleasure of knowing that you're about to begin it again. You might wonder why you need to read something twice, let alone every year of your life. After all, if you read it carefully the first time and discuss it with those around you, as you do every Shabbat, what more can you get from it?

The answer is that as you change, so does the Torah. Every new experience in your life helps you to see and hear something new in the Torah. This is why it is still up to date for the Jewish people, even though it is so old. The *Talmud* explains further what else it might mean, but this is not the last word. Every time someone reads the Torah, another new meaning unfolds. All the meanings of the Torah are there, hidden, waiting to be found. So the joy of Simhat Torah stems from these discoveries. As you learn more about yourself, you find more in the Torah, and the more you find, the closer you come to knowing yourself. That is why the Torah is called the Tree of Life.

A scribe repairing a Torah scroll by
going over faded letters   BILL ARON

Jewish tradition depends upon learning. Many prayers begin: "Our God and God of our ancestors . . ." Why not just "Our God" or just "God of our ancestors"? Why both? The rabbis explained that it meant every person must remember the past but must choose the laws of the Torah for himself or herself. The only way you can choose freely, the tradition says, is by studying and learning, so that you can decide for yourself.

All Jewish parents have the responsibility of teaching their children Torah—and learning Torah means more than just studying Bible stories; it means learning how to lead a good life. The Torah teaches that the world is imperfect; it needs human beings to repair it. The Torah leads the way. Yet Simhat Torah is not a time for study or learning. It's simply a day to joyfully celebrate the past year, which has been spent well in the study of Torah.

On the eve of Simhat Torah, most synagogues are
wonderfully alive and noisy. Disorder is the order of the
day. Children come to synagogue with brightly colored
flags topped with apples, which symbolize the harvest.
Many flags have the following inscription in Hebrew:
"Be joyful and rejoice in the rejoicing of the Lord."
Sometimes people hollow out an apple and place a can-
dle inside it to make a lantern. Then they spear the
apple on the end of the flagpole. This is the one time
when parents don't insist that children sit quietly in
their seats and listen to the rabbi. Instead, they are en-
couraged to use their energy for the *Hakafot*, the circlings of the synagogue with the Torah.

After certain passages are read from the Torah, every
Torah in the synagogue (a wealthy synagogue may have
as many as fifteen) is taken from the *aron ha-kodesh*, the
holy ark, and danced with around the synagogue. Everyone who wishes to carry a Torah does so. The children

Polish 19th-century
Simhat Torah flag
THE JEWISH MUSEUM

follow the Torahs with flags and apples.

The Torah is more than a book; it is a beloved object. It takes a whole year for a Torah to be handwritten by a scribe. Every letter and mark, which must be perfect, is written on sheepskin with ink and pen. Those who hold the Torah and remove it from the ark treat the Torah as a precious object. If they drop it accidentally, they must fast for a time. When the Torah circles the congregation, the people eagerly stretch out their hands to touch it. Then they kiss their fingertips. Those who wear prayer shawls touch the Torah with the corner of the shawl. When a Torah finally wears out, it is never thrown away. It is given a proper burial. All these customs reflect the central place of this holy book in Jewish life.

On Simhat Torah morning, the person honored by being picked to read the last portion of the Torah is called the *hatan Torah,* the bridegroom of the Torah, and the person who reads the beginning is the *hatan Bereshit,* the bridegroom of Genesis. The mood of the day is like the joyful feeling of a wedding. Just as the bride in a Jewish wedding circles the groom seven times, the Torah circles the congregation seven times.

The Torah ends with the end of the forty-year wandering. As soon as this last portion is read, the first book of the Torah, called *Bereshit,* or *Genesis,* is read. There is no pause between the reading of the last and the first portion, because the study of Torah never ends. At the end of the service, the children come up to the Torah for the last section of the reading. A few adults hold a tallit over them. The children say a blessing before and after the reading to thank God for the gift of the Torah.

Reading of the Torah during Simhat Torah; the children are saying a blessing over the Torah.   BILL ARON

4

CELEBRATIONS OLD AND NEW

Whoever fasts on Sukkot is called a sinner.

TALMUD

Sukkot was once the most exciting and most celebrated Jewish holiday. Three thousand years ago it was simply called *he-Hag*, "the Holiday." There was no need to say more, because everyone knew which one it was. When Solomon's Temple, the most glorious house of God, was finished, the Jews dedicated it on Sukkot. It was the grandest holiday because it was the one time of year when farmers could relax for eight days. They had harvested their crops, and it was too soon to plant for the following year.

One thousand years later, *Judah Maccabee* rededicated the Temple for the first *Hanukkah* celebration. Some scholars think that the reason Hanukkah lasts for eight days is that the Maccabees were really celebrating a late Sukkot: They were too busy fighting the Syrians in

19th-century German wooden, hand-painted sukkah, at the Israel Museum ISRAEL MUSEUM, JERUSALEM

October, so they delayed the celebration until after their victory. They marched with palm leaves on that first Hanukkah or late Sukkot.

In the days of the Temple, Jews journeyed to Jerusalem every year on Passover, *Shavuot,* and Sukkot. These were called the "pilgrimage festivals." If a farmer was only able to make one of the trips, it would be the one in honor of Sukkot. It often took weeks to reach Jerusalem, but the hardships of the trip were offset by joyous singing and talking among the pilgrims. They carried full baskets of fruit and grain, which they brought to the Temple as an offering. The first view of Jerusalem from the hills thrilled the travelers. With no trouble they spotted the white marble Temple glistening with gold. When they arrived at the gates of the city, they were greeted by music. Then they marched to the Temple and handed their baskets to the high priest.

Besides the agricultural offerings, there were seventy animal sacrifices on Sukkot, more than on any other holiday. The sacrifices were a gift to God. Each one represented a nation, because according to the Torah, there are seventy nations in the world. The idea of animal sacrifices is hard to understand today, but in ancient times these sacrifices clearly represented this message of Sukkot: that the Messiah will come when all people know that no nation can enjoy happiness until all nations share in it. The Sukkot sacrifices were a way of saying that all people are brothers and sisters.

When the Temple stood, one of the most wonderful ceremonies was the *Bet ha-Sho'evah*, the water-drawing ceremony. On every day of the holiday, except for Shabbat, the priests filled a gold pitcher with water from the sweet springs of Siloam, a pool near Jerusalem. They carried the pitcher up the hill to the altar, where thousands of people in the center court watched the water

The Temple in ancient Jerusalem   SKIRBALL MUSEUM

כי ביתי בית תפלה יקרא לכל העמים

QUIA DOMUS MEA DOMUS ORATIONIS VOCABITUR CUNCTES POPULIS

being poured. At night they celebrated with torch dances. In the center courtyard, the people watched the high priest light huge gold candlesticks with wicks made from the priests' old clothes. People who witnessed this ritual wrote that you could see the light anywhere in Jerusalem. After the lighting, men worthy of the honor danced with torches around the candlesticks while musicians played the flute, harp, and lyre. The ceremony sometimes went on until dawn. The rabbis said that until you've been to a water-drawing ceremony, you have not seen joy.

By the eighteenth and nineteenth centuries, when most of the Jewish people lived in Eastern Europe, it took real faith and imagination to celebrate Sukkot. The Jews were no longer farmers, for they couldn't even own land. Their lives were so poor and miserable that it must have been hard for them to celebrate a holiday that insists upon joy. But for those ghetto Jews, the building of a sukkah was more than a biblical commandment, more than a way of remembering history. It was a preparation for the time that the Jews would return to their homeland of Israel, where once again they would have their own farms for growing and harvesting. When they returned to Israel, their lives would not be fragile, like the sukkah. But in Europe they never knew what hardship would happen next. Europe was like a temporary dwelling that they had to inhabit until they reached their permanent homeland. So for them, building a sukkah was as much a reminder of the future as it was of the past.

The European Jews' sukkot were usually built against a wall, and the children stayed home from school in order to help with the building. Eastern Europe is cold, and its climate is very different from Israel's, so there were no palm branches for the sekhakh. Instead, they used pine branches, which gave off a lovely fragrance. The walls were usually white sheets that were hung on wooden frames and decorated with fruits and flowers.

Since the lulav and etrog could only be gotten from Israel, very few Jews could afford their own. Usually five or six families shared one set of arba'ah minim, and the children profited by this arrangement. They carried the lulav and etrog to the person whose turn it was to bless the arba'ah minim. Sometimes a whole shtetl had only one lulav and one etrog, and these were treated like priceless treasures. All children would follow the lucky child who carried the arba'ah minim from house to house every morning for the special Sukkot blessing. When the person who received the lulav and etrog opened the door, there were sometimes as many as fifty

18th-century German
paper-cut decoration
for a sukkah
ISRAEL MUSEUM,
JERUSALEM

Blessing the arba'ah minim during the Israeli War of
Independence, 1948   ZIONIST ARCHIVES AND LIBRARY

children standing there. They would all be invited in for
tea and cookies. The hardship of not having one's own
arba'ah minim became a happy adventure for everyone.
This tradition continues today in synagogues where
those who have their own lulav and etrog share with
those who don't.

Even during the Holocaust, Jews found ways to celebrate Simhat Torah. One inmate in a concentration
camp discovered a Torah that the Nazis had stolen. He
wound the scroll around his chest and ran back to his
barracks. On Simhat Torah he and his fellow prisoners,
wearing rags and so weak that they could barely stand,
took turns holding the Torah as they circled a bed for
the Hakafot.

By the end of World War II, many of the surviving
Jews left Europe and moved to Israel. Besides the mira-

cle of their survival, there was the miracle of their renewed spirit in this new land. They rediscovered their capacity for joy and hope, and so Sukkot had special meaning for these survivors in Israel.

The days between Yom Kippur and Sukkot are festive in Israel. Everyone is busy buying the arba'ah minim and building sukkot. Jerusalem's main market looks like a carnival, with many people carefully selecting the most stately lulav and the lumpiest lemon-shaped etrog they can afford. In addition to the many lulav and etrog stands, there are also portable sukkot for sale, branches for the sekhakh, and special pictures to decorate the sukkah.

The Israeli sekhakh is usually made of carob tree branches and oleander entwined with palm branches— the same sekhakh that was used in Israel two thousand years ago. The tasty carob fruit hangs between the colorful oleander flowers. The walls of many sukkot are decorated with fine rugs and special paintings that are meant only for this holiday.

In Jerusalem, a prize is awarded for the most beautiful sukkah in the city. Because there are Jews in Jerusalem who come from all over the world, there is a variety of different sukkot and customs. *Kurdish* Jews sit on pillows around a low table in the sukkah, while *Sephardic* Jews prepare a fancy chair for the Ushpizin. They cover it with fine cloth and place sacred books on it. All these customs reflect the wish to fulfill the mitzvah of making the frail sukkah beautiful.

Most people in Jerusalem live in apartments, so many of them build their sukkot on balconies. Others build them in small yards, on roofs, or on sidewalks. The sekhakh must not have anything over it, not even a tree, so apartment buildings in Israel have balconies without overhangs. Each balcony is open to the sky.

Because Israeli schools are closed during Sukkot, many families go on camping trips, but they return in time for Simhat Torah. As mentioned earlier, Shemini Atzeret and Simhat Torah are observed on the same day by Israelis. Simhat Torah is celebrated in much the same way as in America, but the flag and apple have a special meaning: The apple is the fruit of Israel's harvest, and the flag is the flag of Israeli independence.

Soviet Jews are a miracle in modern Jewish history. They are the relatives of the Eastern European Jews who became the majority of the American Jewish community. American Jews have enjoyed religious freedom but the Jews who have remained in Russia have suffered. For generations they have not been allowed to study Torah or pray together. Because of being Jewish, they have been kept from going to college, worshipping freely, and leaving Russia. It is therefore a miracle that Simhat Torah has become the one brave public expression of their Jewishness. Once a year, Soviet Jews affirm their connection to one another, to their history, and to Jews all over the world. Since they cannot escape their Jewishness in Russia, they have made it their strength. Tens of thousands of Jews stand in Red Square in Moscow and sing the Israeli national anthem, *"ha-Tikvah,"* which means "The Hope."

Russian Jews gathered outside Moscow
Synagogue on Simhat Torah   BILL ARON

Building a sukkah in Los Angeles   STEPHANIE SABAR

5
BUILDING A SUKKAH
AND OTHER THINGS

So the people went forth . . . and made themselves booths, everyone upon the roof of his house, and in their courts, and in the courts of the house of God. . . .

NEHEMIAH 8:16

Rosh Hashanah and Yom Kippur feed the mind and spirit; Sukkot nourishes the senses. After the quiet days of contemplation during the High Holy Days, it feels good to pick up a hammer and begin to build a sukkah.

Just because a sukkah is temporary and frail doesn't mean it can't be splendid. It is, after all, a symbol of God's protection. Except for having to follow a few rules from the Talmud, you can let your imagination loose while making the sukkah. For example, it can be built anywhere—some have been built on ships and army jeeps—as long as it is under the open sky. There can be no tree or second story above a sukkah, because the stars should be visible through the sekhakh. The roof covering must be made from plants in their natural state, but cut from their roots. This means that you may not use boards as the sekhakh, but they can be used for support. The sukkah also must be no less than five feet high and no more than thirty feet high.

After Yom Kippur, begin rounding up materials for the sukkah and find a spot to build it. The easiest to build is a sukkah for one person. Ask an adult to help you find a large carton, like the kind a refrigerator comes in, and a sharp knife. Have the open end of the carton facing the sky, and cut a doorway into the lower half of one side. Lay tree branches across the top, and you've got a sukkah. The problem with this sukkah,

however, is that it's too small to share with anyone. An easier solution would be to buy a ready-made sukkah. Some companies sell ones that can be set up without tools in ten minutes! But creating a sukkah yourself is more exciting and fun. It's a chance to build and decorate your own house and feel self-reliant. The more you do to celebrate the holiday, the more it stays in your memory and becomes part of you. Many older people today remember how they helped their own grandfathers build sukkot.

You'll need the following materials to build an eight-by-eight-foot freestanding sukkah, which is cozy but large enough for an eight-day family picnic:

four pieces of two-by-four lumber, cut into eight-foot
    lengths
sixteen pieces of one-by-four lumber, cut into eight-foot
    lengths
"common" nails (the kind with heads that can be pulled
    out easily with a claw hammer when you dismantle
    the sukkah later)
a hammer
a ladder

Industrial-grade wood or number-three pine is good enough for the job.

Lay out the materials and tools, and gather together your building crew. It's a good idea to include an adult in your group in case you run into a problem.

To make your first wall, lay two of the two-by-fours on the ground, and nail four one-by-fours between them as shown in the picture. Be sure the lumber is flat side up. Build a second wall in the same way, and set it aside. Take four more one-by-fours, and hammer them to corners B and D of the first wall to form a right angle. (This is easier to do if the wall is on the ground.) When you've finished hammering the one-by-fours, you should have completed two sides of the sukkah.

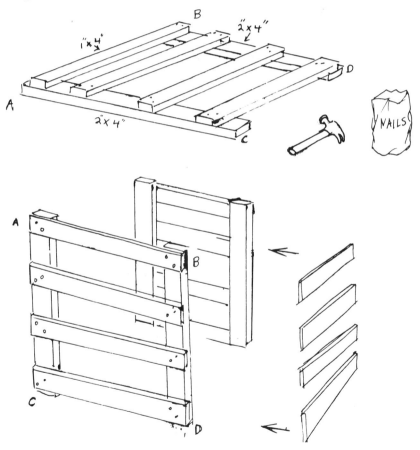

Bring the wall that you set aside earlier over to the unattached ends of the one-by-fours, and hammer them together at right angles to make a third wall. This is simple if one person holds the frame and another person hammers. Now you should have a freestanding sukkah without its sekhakh.

Take the last four one-by-fours and lay them across the top. These boards will support the tree branches. Any branch with leaves on it will do: Pine, palm, and olive branches are possibilities. Even corn stalks make a good sekhakh.

Old sheets, blankets, and bamboo fencing are the easiest materials for completing the walls. Staple any of these coverings tightly to the inside of the frame so they won't flap in the wind. You'll need enough materials for three sides of the sukkah. (When you take down the sukkah, use a staple remover so that you won't harm the sheets or blankets.) The fourth wall can be left open, es-

pecially in a warm climate. But if you want to close it
off, just staple another sheet to that side, leaving one
edge of the sheet free so that you can get in and out. If
you're lucky enough to have some old doors and win-
dows around, they make wonderful walls for the sukkah,
too.

The floor is not important, but if you have an old
piece of carpet, it makes the sukkah fancier. Some people lay sand on the floor to remind them of the desert
wandering.

The sukkah is now ready to decorate. The walls are a
good place to begin. If you plan to use the same sheets
every year, draw pictures right on them with perma-
nent-color marking pens. The Sukkot designs at the end
of this chapter will help you get started. Lean branches

and corn stalks against the walls to give a feeling of autumn. To show the link between the High Holy Days and Sukkot, decorate the walls with New Year's cards and posters of the Ushpizin. The posters can be found in Jewish bookstores, or, if you feel inspired, you can draw your own pictures of the invisible guests. Don't forget the most important adornment of all: the sign that says *Barukh ha-ba,* which means "Blessed be he who comes" or "Welcome" in Hebrew. Here's how it looks in Hebrew:

בָּרוּךְ הַבָּא

The slats holding up the sekhakh make it easy for you to hang overhead decorations. Tie strings around the husks of Indian corn and hang them from a slat. Ornamental gourds are also good to hang because they don't rot quickly. Drive a nail through the top third of the gourd to make two holes. Then remove the nail and thread a string through the nail holes. Attach the gourd to a slat as you did the corn. Fruits and vegetables—such as grapes, pomegranates—and a string of chili peppers or figs also look attractive. But be careful not to overdo your edible decorations. It would be wasteful to use a lot of food that will only be looked at and not eaten. There are many other good ways to decorate.

For a beautiful chain that can be hung from the ceiling or along the walls, all you need are cranberries, peas, a large sewing needle, and strong thread. After threading the needle and knotting the end of the thread, pierce a fresh whole raw cranberry, and push it to the end of the thread with your fingers. Then thread a raw pea the same way. Continue, alternating peas and cranberries, until the thread is strung up to the last inch. Tie a knot at the end, and hang the chain in the sukkah. You could also make a chain from colored construction paper or sheets from old magazines. Cut the paper into one-inch strips and use glue to link them as shown in the picture. They can hang from the ceiling or along the walls.

The following craft is three hundred years old. In the days of the American colonies, Jews decorated their sukkot with yellow, green, purple, and red ribbons pinned to the walls or hanging from the roof as streamers. They also tied the lulav in yards of colored ribbons. Another old idea comes from the Middle East. In Iraq, Jews made figures of birds out of hollowed-out eggs and hung them in memory of members of the family who had died. You can make these birds simply as sukkah decorations, even if they aren't meant for departed relatives.

For this craft, you will need a large raw egg, a straight pin, colored construction paper, scissors, cellophane tape, and white thread. Gently poke a hole through each end of the egg shell. Make one hole slightly larger by moving the pin around the edges of the hole. By blowing through the smaller hole, make the contents of the egg spurt out through the larger hole. Now you have an empty shell, which will be the body of the bird.

Cut a piece of thread two feet long, and tape it to the shell like this:

Cut out the beak, wings, and tail from construction paper. Leave a space on each piece for taping to the shell. Fold the pieces along the dotted lines shown in the illustration, and tape them to the shell. The bird is ready for hanging from the roof of the sukkah.

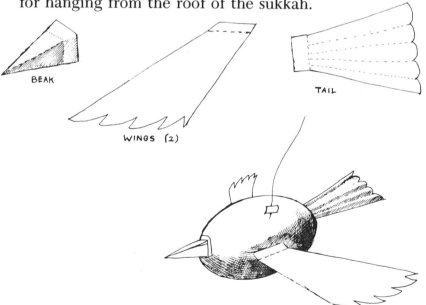

BEAK

WINGS (2)

TAIL

The following craft comes from Mexico. It looks pretty in the sukkah and can be used after Sukkot as a wall or hanging decoration. You need two wooden sticks or twigs, each a foot long, and three or four colors of yarn, each piece three feet long. Cross the sticks of wood to form a plus sign, and glue them to hold. When the glue has dried, tie the sticks together with one piece of yarn, like this:

Turn the sticks over and weave the yarn around the wood like this:

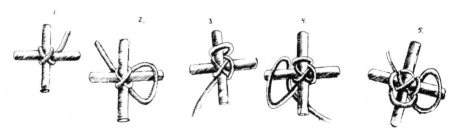

When the yarn is almost used up, tie a piece of yarn of another color to it. Continue this until the sticks are almost entirely covered. Tie the last piece of yarn in a knot around one stick, and leave eight inches of yarn for hanging.

This is another hanging decoration that is a reminder of the "clouds of glory" that protected the Jewish people in the desert. To make a cloud, you will need one sheet of white construction paper; two feet of blue ribbon; two feet of white ribbon; one sheet of red construction paper; and about twenty cotton balls. Cut a large

cloud, in any shape you wish, from the white paper. Cut the blue and the white ribbons into seven pieces of differing lengths and attach them to the cloud with white glue. Alternate the colors. Cut seven six-pointed stars from the red paper. A simple way to do this is to cut fourteen equilateral triangles. Each side of each triangle should be one inch long. Then, with a little glue, attach one triangle on top of another. Glue the stars to the

tips of the ribbons, and glue the cotton balls to the white cloud. Punch a hole near the top of the cloud and put a string through it for hanging.

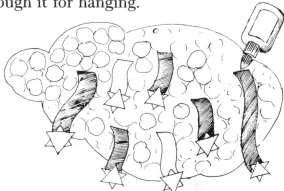

How can you put one sukkah inside another? It's easy. Make a miniature sukkah to decorate the big sukkah. Using poster paint, paint the bottom of a shoebox green and the walls white or yellow. When the paint is dry, put in a miniature table and chairs from a dollhouse. Cut out tiny fruits and vegetables from construction paper,

and put them on the table. If you have modeling clay, you can use it instead to make attractive fruits. Make a tiny lulav by tying a bunch of grass blades together with a piece of string, and make an etrog from the pit of an orange by painting it yellow. Little dolls, pictures of food cut from magazines, and copies of the Sukkot designs (see page 70) will make the toy sukkah look like the real one. Branches from small shrubs and bushes laid across the top of the shoebox make the sekhakh.

A similar idea for this craft is to build a rustic sturdy sukkah from toy Lincoln Logs. Make it as large as you like—say, about six inches high—and instead of using a pitched roof, lay several flat roof pieces across the top to support a few branches.

A Lincoln Log sukkah   STEPHANIE SABAR

The easiest decoration for the sukkah may be found near your house. Many fruit orchards and pumpkin patches are open in early fall. Sometimes you can pick fruits and vegetables on local farms; otherwise, you can buy them in a store. When you get home, fill a large basket with your harvest of fruit, gourds, pumpkins, or corn. This makes a handsome centerpiece in the sukkah. Spread a few autumn leaves around the basket for color and a delicious fragrance.

Here are some crafts that are not connected with decorating the sukkah but nevertheless add to the celebration of Sukkot and Simhat Torah. It's important to protect the etrog during the holiday. If the pittum falls off, you can no longer use it. A wonderful variety of etrog holders have been made by Jews all over the world in different times, but the etrog holder in this craft could only be made today.

Silver etrog box, Vienna, 1870

THE JEWISH MUSEUM

Most supermarkets sell panty hose in containers that look like eggs. If you don't need the panty hose, maybe you can persuade someone in your family to buy them, because their containers make perfect etrog holders. Put some cotton inside both halves of the "egg" to cushion the etrog. Paint the egg with white glue, then dip the wet egg into a jar filled with grains or dried vegetables such as corn, barley, or split peas. The entire surface of the egg should be covered with grain after the dipping. Allow it to dry for at least two hours before using.

Here is a quickly and easily made flag for Simhat Torah. You can use the flag of Israel (see the design page) or make your own design. You can use Sukkot symbols, but be sure to include the most important Simhat Torah symbol—the Torah. Take a piece of white cotton fabric that is nine by twelve inches. Cut out designs for the flag on a piece of colored fabric and glue them to the white piece. Staple the flag to an eighteen-inch-long thin stick. (Most toy and hobby stores carry such sticks.) Be sure to leave enough room at the top for the apple lantern.

שמחת תורה

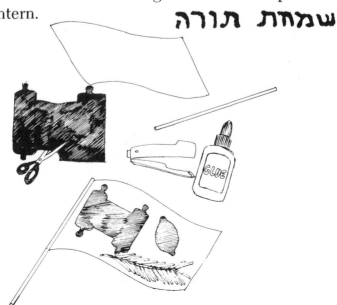

SUKKOT DESIGNS

flag of Israel

Torah

David's harp

Star of David

sukkah

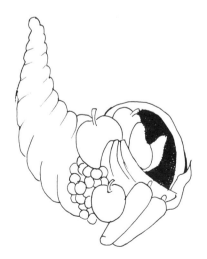

cornucopia

lulav and etrog

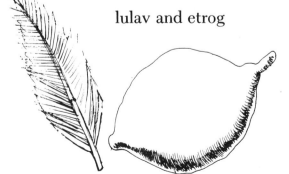

Even though each holiday has its own customs, the festivals of the year are linked to one another because together they celebrate the history of the Jewish people. The tradition is to carry part of one holiday to the next. An example of this is to begin building the sukkah the night of Yom Kippur. In the same way, the lulav is saved to sweep away the bread crumbs of Passover in the spring. The etrog, too, can be saved, because it never rots. It just grows smaller and harder, and it turns black with age. It holds its fragrance for years. After Sukkot, put cloves into the etrog by first piercing the fruit with a toothpick. Then hang the etrog in a closet, and its fragrance will remind you all year of the pleasure of Sukkot.

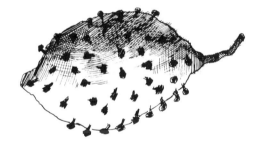

6
party recipes

*Whoever is confident that God has created
every stalk of rye and every drop of water,
tastes the flavor of Paradise in everything
he eats or drinks.*

ISAAC BASHEVIS SINGER, *Reaches of Heaven*

Sukkot is a wonderful time to have a party, since the
focus of the holiday is harvesting food and being hospita-
ble. In addition, the sukkah makes a naturally festive
setting for the long holiday season. Here is a party menu
to celebrate the fall harvest.

STUFFED PUMPKIN

Cut a circle, 6 inches in diameter, in the top of a pumpkin. Since you need a sharp knife and a fair amount of
muscle to do this, make sure an adult is around to help.
Lift the "lid" off and, with a spoon, remove all the pulp
and seeds from the inside. Set aside the pumpkin.

With your fingers, separate the seeds from the pulp. Wash the seeds in a colander until they are free of remaining pulp. Spread them on a cookie sheet covered with aluminum foil. Lightly salt the seeds with kosher (coarse) salt or plain salt. Roast the seeds in a preheated oven at 350° F. (175° C.) for fifteen minutes. You can eat them hot or cold.

While the seeds are roasting, line the inside of the pumpkin with aluminum foil. When the seeds are cool, mix them with nuts and raisins, and put the mixture into the pumpkin. Set this in the sukkah for munching before dinner.

CRANBERRY HALLAH

Hallah is an egg bread that sweetens every Jewish holiday and Shabbat. Here is a recipe for a colorful and tasty
variety.

1 cup fresh cranberries
½ cup frozen apple juice concentrate
1 cup (¼ liter) warm water (98° F. or 36.7° C.)
1 package dry yeast
2 tablespoons sugar
1½ teaspoons salt
2 tablespoons oil
3 eggs
3½ cups (490 grams) white flour

Cut the cranberries in half, put them in a bowl, and
pour in the apple juice concentrate. Let this stand for an
hour. Pour a cup of warm water into a large bowl. Add
the yeast and stir until it is dissolved. Add the sugar, salt,
and oil to yeast mixture and stir until blended. Add two
eggs and beat slightly until they are mixed evenly.
Slowly sprinkle in 3 cups of the flour, stirring it into the
liquid as you do. Sprinkle the remaining ½ cup flour on a
board, and dump the dough onto it. This is the kneading
part. Rub a little flour on your hands, and punch a hole
in the middle of the dough. Then take the dough and
fold it over the hole. Punch it down again. Repeat this
punching and folding for three minutes. Then put the
dough back into the mixing bowl. Cover the bowl with a
damp cloth, and let the dough rise for two hours.

Drain the cranberries in a colander or sieve, and add
them to the dough. Mix and knead the dough until the

cranberries are evenly distributed throughout the dough. A hallah is usually shaped into an oval braid, but on Sukkot it takes even fancier shapes: a key to open heaven, a ladder for prayers to climb and reach heaven, and a circle to signify the cycle of the year.

Here is how to make a round hallah: Flour the board again and put the dough on it. It should be twice as big as it was when you first put it in the bowl. Punch it down and begin to shape it into a long snake, about 18 inches long. Place the dough on a cookie sheet. Hold one end in place and with your other hand, coil the rest of the dough in a circle around that end. The center should be higher than the outer circle, so that the hallah looks round and turbanlike when you're done.

Separate the white from the yolk of the third egg and save the yolk. Dip your fingers into the yolk and smear it over the dough. This will make the crust shiny after the hallah has baked.

Bake the dough in a preheated oven at 350° F. (175° C.) for 45 minutes. Take the cookie sheet out of the oven, lift the bread off, and tap the bottom of the bread. If it sounds hollow, it's done.

STUFFED ARTICHOKES

This is a filling main course for four hungry people.

4 large artichokes
1 stick of butter
2 green onions, chopped fine
1 cup chopped mushrooms
1 cup shredded mild Cheddar cheese
½ teaspoon salt
½ cup bread crumbs
2 eggs, beaten
½ cup sour cream
grated cheese

Clip off the artichoke tops (the sharp thorny parts of the leaves) with scissors. Put the artichokes in a large pot with two inches of water and cook them over a low flame for an hour. You may have to add more water at some point to keep them from burning. The artichokes are done when the outside leaves can be easily pulled off.

When the artichokes have cooled, spread the leaves and remove the fuzzy center from inside each artichoke. It will come out easily with a soup spoon. Don't cut out the bottom of the artichoke, because that part is delicious. When you've hollowed all the artichokes, set them aside while you make the stuffing.

Put two tablespoons of butter and green onions into a frying pan, and cook them over a low flame for three minutes. Add the mushrooms and cook for two minutes more. Remove the pan from the stove, and put the mixture into a medium-size bowl. Add the Cheddar cheese (setting aside a little for sprinkling on the top later), salt, and bread crumbs. Mix the eggs and sour cream together; then add them to the mixture.

Stuff the artichokes with the mixture and sprinkle the remaining cheese on top. Put them in a preheated oven and bake at 400° F. (204° C.) for a half hour.

When you're ready to serve the artichokes, melt the rest of the butter in a little custard dish and set it on the table. This is how you eat an artichoke: Pull out a leaf, dip it in butter, and slide it between your teeth. Throw away the remains of the leaf. It's a good idea to serve artichokes on big plates that have room for all the discarded leaves.

BULL'S-EYE SANDWICHES

If you can't find artichokes, this recipe is an easy substitute for a main course. It will serve four people.

4 pieces of whole wheat bread
½ stick butter
4 eggs

Lay the four pieces of bread on a flat surface. Press the open end of a water glass into the center of each piece so that you remove a circle from each, leaving a hole. (Store the circles separately, since you won't need them again in this recipe.) Melt half the butter in a large frying pan, and put into the pan two of the bread slices with holes. Crack an egg and drop it carefully into one hole. Repeat for the other hole. Cover the pan with a lid and let the eggs cook for two minutes over a medium flame. Remove the "bull's eyes" from the pan with a spatula. Add the rest of the butter and the last two pieces of bread, and follow the recipe again.

DATE BREAD

This dessert may remind you of the lulav, because the fruit of that plant is the date.

> 2 cups white flour
> ½ cup brown sugar
> 2 teaspoons baking powder
> 1 teaspoon salt
> 1 egg, beaten
> 1 cup milk
> 2 tablespoons butter
> ¾ cup chopped dates

In a large bowl, mix together the flour, sugar, baking powder, and salt. Add the beaten egg and the milk to the flour mixture. Melt the butter in a saucepan, and blend it into the mixture. Mix in the dates. Place the dough in a greased bread pan and bake in a preheated oven at 350° F. (175° C.) for 40 minutes. Or you can bake the bread in small all-metal 8-ounce greased juice cans. These make nice cylindrical loaves that can be sliced into pretty round pieces. Bake each can for 30 minutes.

FRUIT PUNCH

This drink takes no time to make and is both healthful and refreshing.

> *1 cup pineapple juice*
> *1 cup cranberry juice*
> *1 cup orange juice*
> *sprigs of fresh mint*

Mix the ingredients together and pour into glasses. Garnish with a sprig of fresh mint.

7

SUKKOT FUN

Here are some puzzles and mind benders for you to fig-
ure out under a leafy sekhakh. The answers start on page
84.

SUKKOT RIDDLES

1. What's yellow, lumpy, and has red spots?
2. What is in the middle of Sukkot?
3. What time is it when a hurricane hits the sukkah?
4. What did the girl tell her friend when she gave him a
   new record album?
5. What did one wall of the sukkah say to the other
   wall?

SCRAMBLED WORDS

These words have something to do with Sukkot. Can you
unscramble them?

GRETO
RYEMLT
VICEGORN
REDSET
SAVTEHR

DOUBLE CROSS

These double word crosses are all about Sukkot and Simhat Torah. The objects in each cross have something to do with one another. Here is an example:

Now, try these:

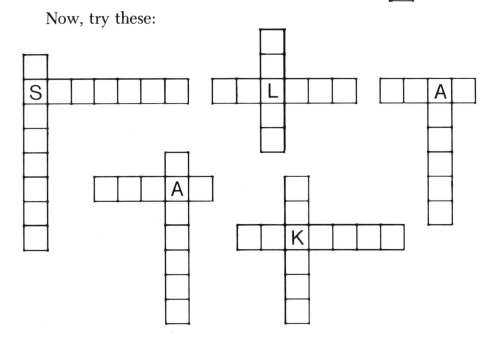

WORD COUNT

How many words can you make from the letters of the word *Hospitality*? (No proper nouns, two-letter words, or plurals are allowed.)

WORD SEARCH

In each sentence below, a word related to Sukkot is hidden. Can you find it? There's a clue in parentheses at the end of each sentence.

1. He will own a computer after his bar mitzvah. (arba'ah minim)
2. Do you have proof?   (part of sukkah)
3. I saw all of you in the sukkah.   (part of sukkah)
4. The magic wand erased his mistake.   (search)

MAGIC BOX

What does this number box have to do with Sukkot?

9	12	17	2
16	3	8	13
4	19	10	7
11	6	5	18

CODE

This code hides the most important message of Sukkot. Can you break the code and decipher the message?

Y oush allha ven ot h ingb utj oy.

ANSWERS

RIDDLES

1. An etrog with measles.
2. The letter K.
3. Time to leave the sukkah.
4. I hope lulav it! (I hope you love it!)
5. I'll meet you at the corner.

SCRAMBLED WORDS

ETROG
MYRTLE
COVERING
DESERT
HARVEST

DOUBLE CROSS

```
                        L           S
U               H       U           U
SHARING   TORAH   WILLOW   SEKHAKH   FLAG
H               K       A           K        P
P               A       V           A        P
I               F                   H        L
Z               O                            E
I               T                            S
N
```

WORD COUNT

ail	sit	alit	ship	aptly	pistol
apt	sly	alop	shop	hoist	polish
ash	sop	also	shot	hotly	postal
asp	sot	alto	silt	laity	spoilt
has	spy	atop	slap	pasty	spotty
hat	sty	hail	slay	patsy	
hay	tap	halt	slip	pithy	
hip	thy	hash	slit	posit	hospital
his	tip	hasp	slop	potty	
hit	top	hilt	slot	salty	
hop	toy	holy	soap	shalt	hostility
hot		host	soil	spilt	
its		lash	spat	splat	
lap		last	spit	split	
lay		lisp	spot	spoil	
lip		list	stay	stilt	
lit		lost	stop	tipsy	
lop		opal	tail	toast	
lot		pail	that	total	
oat		past	this		
oil		path	tilt		
pal		pita	toil		
pat		pith			
pay		pity			
pit		play			
ply		plot			
pot		ploy			
sap		posh			
sat		post			
say		posy			
shy		sail			
sip		salt			

WORD SEARCH

1. He will own a computer after his bar mitzvah.
2. Do you have proof?
3. I saw all of you in the sukkah.
4. The magic wand erased his mistake.

MAGIC BOX

Each column of numbers adds up to forty vertically, horizontally, and diagonally. The Jews wandered for forty years in the desert.

CODE

This code doesn't change the letters or the words, only the spaces between the words. So the code reads:

You shall have nothing but joy.

AFTERWORD

When I was growing up, I thought that Sukkot was too good to be true. I got to camp out right in my own backyard; my family had a chance to be "rough and ready."

Inside the fragile sukkah, I was never afraid when the wind blew. The fact that my family and I were all together made me feel safe. Now that I am grown, I still feel that way. Each of us, despite our education and the use of modern machines, remains as fragile as a sukkah in the wind.

But if we all, as fellow travelers on earth, stand together, we can feel strong and safe. Sukkot, an ancient holiday once celebrated by a primitive people, still resounds with powerful meaning: It is a time to remember and to rejoice in the interdependence of all living things.

APPENDIX

Blessing for lighting the candles:

Praised are You, Lord our God, Ruler of the Universe, Who has taught us the way of holiness through Your commandments, which include the mitzvah of kindling the [Shabbat and the] Festival lights.

Blessing over the wine (kiddush):

Praised are You, Lord our God, King of the Universe, Who creates fruit of the vine.

Praised are You, Lord our God, King of the Universe, Who has chosen and distinguished us by sanctifying our lives with His commandments. Lovingly have You given us [this Shabbat and] this Sukkot, a day for holy assembly and for recalling the Exodus from Egypt. Your faithful word endures forever. Praised are You, Lord, King of all the earth, who sanctifies [Shabbat,] the people Israel and the festive seasons.

Blessing over food (ha-motzi):

Praised are You, O Lord, Who gives us food from the earth.

GLOSSARY

ARAVOT—Willows; one of the four species.

ARBA'AH MINIM—The four species or plants (etrog, lulav, aravot, hadasim) used during Sukkot.

ARON HA-KODESH—The holy ark in which the Torah is kept.

BA'AL SHEM TOV—The great Hasidic master who lived in the eighteenth century.

BARUKH HA-BA—Hebrew words for "Welcome"; they literally mean "Blessed be he who comes."

BERESHIT—Genesis, the first book of the Torah; the word literally means "In the beginning."

BET HA-SHO'EVAH—The ancient water-drawing celebration performed during Sukkot.

C.E.—Common Era. Christians use the term A.D. (Anno Domini, which means "in the year of the Lord").

ECCLESIASTES—One of the books of the Bible; it is read during Sukkot.

ETROG—Citron; one of the four species.

GENESIS—The first book of the Torah; also called Bereshit.

GESHEM—Hebrew word for rain, which is prayed for on She-mini Atzeret.

HADASIM—Myrtle; one of the four species.

HAG HA-ASIF—"Festival of the Ingathering," another name for the Sukkot holiday.

HAKAFOT—The circlings of the synagogue made while holding the Torah during Simhat Torah.

HALLAH (hallot, pl.)—Holiday bread.

HALLEL—Hebrew word meaning "praise"; the name of the ceremony in which Psalms 113–118 are recited on certain holidays, including Sukkot.

HA-MOTZI—Blessing said over food.

HANUKKAH—Dedication; the Feast of Dedication or the Festival of Lights.

HASIDIM—The fervent mystical Jews of eighteenth-century Eastern Europe.

HATAN BERESHIT—"Bridegroom of Genesis," the one who reads the beginning of the Torah on Simhat Torah.

HATAN TORAH—"Bridegroom of the Torah," the one who reads the last part of the Torah on Simhat Torah.

HA-TIKVAH—Israeli national anthem; "The Hope."

HE-HAG—Hebrew for "the Holiday," another name for Sukkot.

HIGH HOLY DAYS—The most solemn and holy days of the Jewish year, Rosh Hashanah and Yom Kippur.

HOL HA-MOED—The five middle days of Sukkot, which are half-holidays.

HOSHANAH—Hebrew for "O Save Us!", sung during the circling ceremony on Hoshanah Rabbah.

HOSHANAH RABBAH—Seventh day of Sukkot.

HOSHANOT—The recitations that accompany the circling of the synagogue by the congregation while holding the four species.

JUDAH MACCABEE—A great Jewish soldier who, with his

band of followers, defeated the Syrians and rededicated the Temple in 165 B.C.E. The Feast of Hanukkah celebrates this event.

KIDDUSH—Blessing over wine said on Shabbat and festivals.

KOSHER—Prepared for use according to Jewish law.

KURDISH—Of or from Kurdistan, a part of Iraq.

LEVIATHAN—A gigantic supernatural sea creature.

LEVITE—One of the families from which all Jews are descended.

LULAV—The date palm; one of the four species.

MAIMONIDES—A great medieval philosopher (1135–1204); one of the greatest Hebrew scholars.

MATZAH (matzot, pl.)—Unleavened bread eaten during Passover.

MITZVAH (mitzvot, pl.)—Good deed; rule or commandment that Jews believe God gave them to lead a good life.

MYSTIC—A person who believes in special, mysterious, religious meanings that go beyond external ritual.

PASSOVER—Spring holiday that celebrates Moses' leading the Jews out of slavery in Egypt.

PITTUM—The blossom end of the etrog.

ROSH HASHANAH—Head of the Year; New Year.

SEKHAKH—The leafy covering that forms the roof of the sukkah.

SEPHARDIC—Characteristic of the Sephardim, Jews who were expelled from Spain in 1492 and who then resettled in the Middle East.

SHABBAT—The Jewish Sabbath, the holiest day of the week, celebrated from Friday evening till Saturday evening; the day of rest and completion.

SHAVUOT—A spring harvest holiday that celebrates the giving of the Ten Commandments.

SHEKEL—A coin used in nineteenth-century Eastern Europe.

SHEKHINAH—The Divine Presence (feminine).

SHEMINI ATZERET—Eighth day of Sukkot, celebrated with much joy.

SHTETL—Eastern European Jewish village.

SIMHAT TORAH—"Rejoicing in the Torah"; the holiday celebrating the completion of the Torah reading and the beginning of the new readings.

SUKKAH (sukkot, pl.)—A hut or little house that Jews use during Sukkot.

SUKKAT SHALOM—The great Shelter of Peace, in which it is hoped all the people of the world will some day sit together.

SUKKOT—Feast of Booths; the autumn harvest festival beginning on 15 Tishri.

TA'AM—Hebrew for "taste" and "common sense."

TABERNACLES—Booths or huts.

TALLIT (tallitot, pl.)—Prayer shawl.

TALMUD—The body of Jewish civil and ceremonial law.

TESHUVAH—Returning to God; self-examination.

TIKKUN—A special evening of study on Hoshanah Rabbah.

TISHRI—Seventh month of the year in the Hebrew calendar; the month in which Rosh Hashanah, Yom Kippur, and Sukkot fall.

TORAH—The first five books of the Bible; guidance, direction; also called the tree of life.

TZEDAKAH—Giving to those in need; justice.

USHPIZIN—Invisible guests who are invited to visit the sukkah.

YIZKOR—A memorial service to remember relatives and friends who have died.

YOM KIPPUR—Day of Cleansing, Purification; Day of Atonement.

ZEMAN SIMHATENU—"Season of Our Joy," another name for Sukkot.

ZOHAR—The chief book of Jewish mystical teaching.

SUGGESTED
READINGS

Theodore Gaster. *Festivals of the Year.* New York: William Morrow & Co., 1972.

Philip Goodman. *The Sukkot Anthology.* Philadelphia: Jewish Publication Society of America, 1973.

Hayyim Schauss. *The Jewish Festivals.* New York: Schocken Books, 1978.

Richard Siegel. *The First Jewish Catalog.* Philadelphia: Jewish Publication Society of America, 1973.

Leo Trepp. *The Complete Book of Jewish Observance.* New York: Behrman House/Summit Books, 1980.

INDEX

Adam and Eve, 18
American Jews, 52, 62
Animal sacrifices, 47
Aravot (willow sprigs), 17, 18, 89
  symbolism of, 19
Arba'ah minim (four species), 16,
  20, 50, 89
  Eastern Europe, 49–50
  Hoshanah Rabbah, 36, 90
  Israel, 12, 51
  symbolism of, 19–25
Aron ha-kodesh, 42, 89
Artichokes, stuffed, 76–77
Atzeret, 38

Ba'al Shem Tov, 15–16, 89
Barukh ha-ba, 61, 89
Bereshit, 43, 89
Bet ha-Sho'evah (water-drawing
  ceremony), 47–48, 89
Bible, 16
Bird decorations, 62–63
Blessings, 88
  illustrated, 12
Bread
  date bread recipe, 79
  hallah, 30
  hallah recipe, 74–75
Bull's-eye sandwiches recipe, 78

Calendar
  history of, 12–13
  Sukkot, 11, 12
Carob tree branches, 51
Centerpieces, 67
Citron (etrog). See Etrog (citron)
Cloud construction, 65
Code game, 83, 86
Concentration camps, 50
Cranberry hallah, 74–75

Date bread, 79
David, 32
Decorations, 60–67
  designs for, 70
Double cross puzzle, 82, 84

Eastern European Jews, 48–50
Ecclesiastes, 16, 89
Egypt, 13
Eliezer, Rabbi, 13–14
Etrog (citron), 18, 25, 68, 89
  Eastern European celebrations,
    49, 50
  Hoshanah Rabbah, 36, 90
  Israeli celebrations, 51
  preservation of, 71
  symbolism of, 19, 21, 22, 23, 24
    25
Etrog holders, 68

Feast of Tabernacles, 10
Festival of the Ingathering
  (Hag ha-Asif), 14–15, 90
Flag construction, 69, 70
Four species. See Arba'ah minim;
  entries under names of species
Fruit punch recipe, 80

Games and puzzles, 81–86
  code game, 83, 86
  double cross, 82, 84
  magic box, 83, 86
  riddles, 81, 84
  scrambled words, 81, 84
  word count, 82, 85
  word search, 83, 86
Garden of Eden, 18
Geshem (prayer), 38
  See also Prayers